KEYBOARD INTERCOURSE

Keyboard Intercourse

Charles Plymell

Edited by Benito Vila
Prelude by Mike Watt

Bottle of Smoke Press
2023

Keyboard Intercourse © 2023 by Charles Plymell
Introduction © 2023 by Benito Vila
Prelude © 2023 by Mike Watt
Cover photo © 2023 by the Estate of Allen Ginsberg
Rear Cover Collage © 2023 by the Estate of Mary Beach

ISBN-13:   978-1-954718-06-7 (Paper)
           978-1-954718-07-4 (Hardcover)

Published by:
Bottle of Smoke Press
8 Bridle Way
Wappingers Falls, NY 12590
bill@bospress.net

I Love This Man, a Prelude by Mike Watt

Charley Plymell inspires me, brought a fourth opera out of me by bringing the libretto. Word man. Collage man + picture man = put a paragraph together w/pictures, man. Channel it, build a canal on it. Get it. Charley gave me a shirt. I love this shirt, love to wear this shirt Charley gave me. It lets me breathe! It can breathe! Charley's threads looking for needles in my head, the way I hear his writing, using my eyes to see them for the words they are. I think of the Italian for "the focused glance" cuz I had cause to think of it before but now…just like meaningless meaning useless, ok, kind of like. Charley's been in my boat (now donated), he's seen the piss bottle. Well, it seems lighthouses end up either beacons or warners when really put to use, correct? I did another bass recording to Charley's stuff, his voice, for Brother Sam to finish and we'll call it "Sideways Eight" for Charley cuz he deserves it. In the meantime, I get emails from Charley, ever since Grant Hart introduced me to him at a poetry trip Byron Coley put on in West Mass. Sometimes, they got the best poems in them he's written. Also, observations he digs sharing. Trippy way to make conversation but Charley lots of the time can get them really interesting for me and so I'm grateful for bumrush of word-such, they're like little ostinatos sometimes and they can get the bass part of my mind big time motivated. I couldn't be more grateful, truly…I love this man.

on bass, watt

PS. I think it's "lo squardo focalizzato", or is it "occhiata"?

Grant Hart, Mike Watt, & Charles Plymell at Byron Coley's Yod Space in Florence, Massachusetts, November 18, 2007. Photo by Bill Roberts.

Who, What, Now: An Introduction

In another era, Charles Plymell might have been referred to as a storyteller, or maybe as Lucretius, Herodotus, Descartes, Kant or Yeats. An independent small press publisher since the early 1960s, Plymell has earned a following in international literary circles as a thoroughly modern poet (his work appearing far and wide since 1955), as the link between the Beats and the Hippies (a tag he's never cared for), and as a godfather of underground comix (having printed the first *Zap* in 1968).

Plymell prides himself on his other "work", digging trenches for gas lines across the American West in the 1950s, handling cargo on the docks in San Francisco in the 1960s, teaching literature and philosophy in East Coast universities and prisons in the 1970s and 1980s, and delivering milk from upstate New York to New York City in the 1990s. Today, in 2023, he says, "I'm 88 years old in April and spend 88% of the time thinking about death."

"Death is a waste of time" is one of Plymell's more recent epiphanies, one in a stream of ideas and stories he shares via email with an appreciative sea of friends. Writing is rarely ever the sole focus of Plymell's mind. The perplexities of life, language and learning are. At 88, he'd prefer to drive a tractor, feed feral cats, read something new, or help a friend in need, than set aside time to type up a new essay or complete a new poetry collection. He's always preferred to be in-the-know and free of the celebrity spotlight, an attitude that puzzled his friend Allen Ginsberg. It's an honest way of life that fits him perfectly, one that's led Plymell to be a sought-after counterculture seer and a teacher of underground "cool". It's also connected him to a Who's Who of creative expression, from Paul Bley, Bob Branaman and Ray Bremser to Andy Warhol, A.D. Winans, and Mike Watt.

A "punk" long before that was ever a term, Plymell is not one for reverence except when it comes to indigenous people, '50s R&B and fast cars. He's quick to call out the boorish, clubby salesmanship he feels is the basis of success for the likes of Ginsberg, Jack Kerouac, Lawrence Ferlinghetti and others, including *The New York Times*, Maya Angelou and Bob Dylan. Plymell questions anything and everything that sets itself aside as being "hot" or "in demand", or anyone and everyone who takes themselves so seriously that they need to be seen or spoken to in a certain way. He and Ginsberg were close friends, but Plymell readily says he preferred the company of William Burroughs, Neal Cassady and Herbert Huncke, like-minded mid-Westerners, who each became a companion and a co-conspirator.

I first met Charley by phone in 2019, staying in touch regularly by email before we finally met in-person in mid-2021. The pandemic had a lot to do with that, but it was his fiery, on-it, thought-provoking email correspondence that led me to wonder if I could piece together a story from what Charley was writing. One draft led to another and, in early 2021, *Of Myth & Men* was published by Bottle of Smoke Press, thanks to the encouragement of nine people whose bits of conversation I included, and the guidance of Charley's wife, Pam, and the book's publisher, Bill Roberts. Poet/photographer and Warhol collaborator Gerard Malanga picked the cover photo: young poet, printer and budding cultural historian Charles Plymell in a tree, circa 1963, gazing towards everything that was coming next.

Charley originally wanted the book's title to be "Keyboard Intercourse", but he relented to our play on the John Steinbeck title, a nod to two of his book titles, *Last of the Moccasins* and *Incognito, Ergo Sum*. The title, *Of Myth & Men*, was also our choice because the narrative was largely about Charley, his mythology and his people. I promised Charley that *Keyboard Intercourse* would be the title of the next email book and here it is, a collage, a cut-up of philosophy, history and poetry that is purely and solely Charles Plymell.

PART PHILOSOPHY

SUBJECT: To combat the GOOGLESOUL

I'd rather be called a "philosopher" now. I think "poet" has no meaning anymore.

Human brains have tangled with the notion that their creator will never be known. They have done everything they can think of...football; wars; building gilded monuments; pro-creation; anything to ward off the notion of "not knowing", anything to not suffer from the unknown. We are not at the end of evolution. Our information technologies can make us into a body, a mind free of agnosticism.

Sometimes, I get an eerie existential feeling that I won't be here. Where will I be, or, what was it that I was and why?

I think my philosophy will continue past my Will and Idea. My dad and I were riding on the prairie one day, and to paraphrase what he said, "Whatever it is that created the whole thing ain't gonna let a little thing like man figure it out, and if he tries, he will just go insane."

The computer (AI) artificial intelligence has delivered enough information for us to re-create ourselves without the question that suffers the unknown. We can even delete the war games that lead a 19-year-old to commit mass shootings, or the need for the cop suicides, like Jesus and Judas cooked up.

Right now, at 87, I'm taking care of 40 or so strays (some are sick and others people have dumped on me because they see me feeding them––the Amerikun Way). I just gave Cheerios to a baby doe in the yard. "Innocent" has a connotative value of creatures that may not have to think of the unknowable, probably, although it's clear they do have personalities.

SUBJECT: Re: The Little Spanish Town Pt. IIA

I like factual relevance to complete the Idea. I taught philosophy at Colgate and a course called "Words and Ideas" at Johns Hopkins. I taught professional writing at George Washington, George Mason, University of Maryland, et al. I turned down two poetry courses at American University, because I'd rather teach substance. "Audience" was key in professional writing. Little details that aren't over-explained were apparent in the likes of William Faulkner, although I'm no expert on fiction. I've tried to pass myself off as song writer.

It's unlikely that Luckys & Camels caused too much illness. They were real tobacco compared to poison in modern cigarettes. Driving along El Camino Real onetime I couldn't help but notice how trashy the highway became when I went past Nixon country.

SUBJECT: Re: LANGUAGE

There were more libraries during time of scribes than now. Words may not matter so much to those who grow up texting and tweeting.

Thurgood Marshall used "Negro". That's good enough for me. Rachel Maddow and three women from Howard were saying it was the most awful word possible. It was used in the census at one time. Of course, it seemed legitimate there, back then. I'm with comedians & musicians from '60s who wanted to use n***** until it wore out, like the way people have learned to say "fuck". The n-word is "illegal" now for younger generation, in any context. I think the control of language, the God of lies (and guns) had everything to do with orange fool getting elected.

I don't think Patti Smith could sing her: "Rock N Roll Nigger" like she did at Bowery Ballroom when Pam and I were Patti and Grant Hart's guests. It was a favorite song of Patti's mother, who was there, too. Patti sang it at the Rock & Roll Hall of Fame when Reverend Al Sharpton was in the crowd.

I was in San Francisco during the Black Panthers' gun march to Reagan's State Capitol in Sacramento and hung out with them, and the Peace & Freedom Party in same building, pre-1966, when hippies were liberating the F-word & its frigging, f'ing acceptable variants. I was at Dean Stockwell's house in the canyon (maybe 1963) when he played James Brown, who was just becoming popular. I think "Black" came a proper designation with James Brown. "Colored" was the term of respect in my day. It was considered "welcoming" and didn't become pejorative until the use of "Colored Only" spread across the South.

If I ever write my semantic study of "W-words", I wanted to conclude with the fact that people will use the acceptable "n-word" to denote a specific referent. That being the case, can it be said we had an n-word president? Is the adjective "colored woman" wrong, but the infinitive, woman of color, right? Abraham Lincoln said something after the Civil War about old wrongs being forgotten...I don't have the quote right here...but clinging to and outlawing bad words has never determined a civilization.

Language and democracy seem in peril now. To misquote Aram Saroyan: "America is not a democracy, it's an economy." Aram originally said, "America is not a culture, it's an economy." America is, and always has been, built on money, most of it illegal, starting with the Roosevelt family's clipper ships running dope.

Black culture seems to be in peril, too. I watched the CNN Juneteenth last night. Awful, except for the woman who did modern dance. I've never seen such music crap in clown suits. Poor Sister Rosetta. poor Ray Charles, poor Nina Simone, poor Aretha Franklin. Is Sly of Sly & The Family Stone still homeless on streets of L.A.?

I watched the CNN show about Greenwood-Tulsa for the second time. I didn't realize the importance of the period, the greatest reparation ever for the United States. The show seemed to be saying that Oklahoma from 1880s to 1905 became "a promised land" for Negroes and Indians, and if they could prove African heritage or a native tribe, they could get 160 acres. One Black woman on the show rightly said that land ownership made all the difference, that that gave them "a place". I need to know more about what happened to cause the massacre. Probably just plain stupid bigotry, and jealousy of their wealth and religion. Coloreds had great churches, theatres, etc. I would love to know which musicians played in Greenwood-Tulsa.

Calling it the "Tulsa Race Riot" seems to euphemistically shift the blame to the Blacks, even the term "race war" has that convenient connotation. I need to do more research and will try the University of Oklahoma Press to see if they published any books of that period. I want know more about the politics and conditions of that time. It's important that people know Oklahoma for more than the "gushers" that is popular history, that the Promised Land of the Good God existed only to have it broken by the Evil God.

I hate baseball & all competitive sports, moneyed endeavors made to keep the population from killing each other. I can hardly shop in Cooperstown when the great bloated cross section of American idiots goes there every summer. Ignorance Tr(i)umps. And now sports are being consumed by their own greed and seem to be giving way to the NRA's "new sport": killing innocence.

SUBJECT: Link Wray and Rumble

Just the beat was banned in the '50s. Not the words. Even though banning the beat didn't change anything. Now they want to ban the bodies.

I can't get past the new Supremes ruling because I can't get past who would think someone's pregnancy is any of their damn business anyway? Is this the greatest ignorant country in the world? Something strange is going on with common sense. Partisan politics. What the f-word!

> Great latent ambiguities of sex and gender
> conundrums solved by a simple condom.
>
> A civilization doomed by gadgets
> no awareness of natural history
> and time is cleared of evidence
> from informational inch worms
> over the cliff and ancient berms.

We need to have a posT rump party and run naked through the woods.

SUBJECT: Scribbling

You are assuming publishing and distribution is like it was in the past. Everything has changed. We are on the cusp of an age never before seen in national consciousness. Must be jelly 'cause jam don't shake like that.

SUBJECT: Re: Is This a Poem?

Don't bother me with gobble de gook. There is no such thing as poetry, only De Gook of Gobble. Cobble that, clodhopper.

The best definition of poetry was what I heard once, but I forget who said it, "Poetry is what poets write."

SUBJECT: Re: space steps into the jeweled indifference

I bought a 1952 Buick Roadmaster in Hollywood at 17 by trading in the new 1952 GMC pickup my dad bought for me. I went to Oregon to visit my sister and ended up driving a dump truck working on rock crusher. I went back to Wichita after working on pipeline out of Flagstaff, Arizona for a while. I was 17, driving across Nevada. I can't understand the 18-year-old in the news this week, who couldn't drive but was able to put together a military arsenal. I was foolish, but the thought of mass killings never entered my mind. I don't know what to say about news.

In Ely, Nevada there was a good Basque restaurant across tracks. They put a jug of wine and bread on the table as soon as anyone sat down. There was a lot of sheep herding in those parts then. Driving alone, it was pitch black. If I turned off car lights, I couldn't see my hand in front of me. And then, there it was: the traditional mother ship, a long cigar shaped thing with illuminations alongside where the traditional saucer shaped craft flew out. The hairs on my neck stood up as they maneuvered. I put the Buick to the floor, got to over a hundred, but they weren't after me and disappeared in "space steps."

In Holcomb, Kansas, I remember my dad talking about the machine gun. It was outlawed immediately by the government when Machine Gun Kelly out gunned the law. The sawed-off shotgun was made illegal, too. They were for killing people. The Feds acted quickly then. That was in the '30s. Too little too late now. Biden wants "cooperation" from the "other party". It ain't no party.

SUBJECT: Re: "Whatever it is that created the whole thing..."

My thesis is that humankind does everything (like wars) because it doesn't know why it is. Have you never wondered about existence itself? Even the young are going with Jesus again. It's the easiest thing. One can accept Him and get a clean slate. Born-again GOPs know this. I grew up with them.

As far as communicating my thesis, human intercourse expects taking "sides". Abortion, which no one talked about in my day except perhaps as gossip, has now become the evening news lead with both sides protesting and rallying in the streets. Isn't that quite insane?

I'm not saying humankind should delete the quest for the Almighty. I'm saying it may delete its quest in its new makeup, maybe in order to save itself from extinction. If you run to Papa Church when the bells ring down the block, you, of course, don't have to think about existence. Ever. It's covered for you. Drink the wine; drink the Kool-Aid. It's all the same thing. I'm agnostic to begin with. I simply don't know.

We all need our "talk" with the unknown. I grew up around the organized religion pitches, like the song line, "Having a little talk with Jesus makes me whole." The cross seems a cumbersome and weighty symbol to carry around. The Indians had it right: chalk it up to the bit that stays unknown. The monarch butterflies probably know as much about it. One thing for sure, things are limited in the human experience and empirical evidence and experience has been usurped by the machine that will be able to re-create us all.

I don't use email like others do. A book was published of my emails (with others' permission, of course) titled *Of Myth & Men*. A first, telling a story through emails. A second one, *Keyboard Intercourse*, is coming out, to replace the man of letters with the man of the mouse. If you are not familiar with connotative/denotative meanings, "intercourse" has a denotative meaning, used in World War Two instructions, not to have "intercourse" with the enemy.

Three more years will pass like a stampede of Mustangs. I will be 90 and probably in a wheel chair. No one cares about old fucks. I spend my waking moments taking care of innocent creatures.

SUBJECT Re: Psychedelics in Retrospect

We took the Sandoz, c1962 in San Francisco. Owsley then made a comparable batch that he put in vitamin pills. Magic mushrooms grew in Golden Gate Park. Justin, Glenn's partner, ate some of those and said the right side of his brain was stimulated. We had peyote in the '50s in Wichita, 50 cents a button, I think. I saw them in a cactus shop in Tucson last time I was there. In my book, I talk of offering a button to black guy who played sax. He took out his handkerchief from vest pocket to handle it, gave it back, saying, "Hunhuh, man!" No way. The Indians around Wichita and other places out West used peyote in religious rites. There was a book I read in '50s about the town in France where Jackie Kennedy's folks were from. The town had gone crazy. Dogs were chewing the bark off trees. They finally traced it to town's baker who was using old flour with ergot for rye bread.

Peyote is medicine alright. It's not for kicks. None of the psychedelics are. Leary was basically a fool, an academic. After he and his cronies gave a presentation at a big hotel lobby in **San Francisco**...at a hefty fee, to thousands of suckers...I remember going up the stairs to an "in crowd" after-party. Alongside him a woman tripped on her long hippie beads. He was next to her and could have offered a hand, but didn't. That would have been a "normal" reaction. I helped her up to see if she was hurt, while he "dropped out".

Manners and ethics are lost in an ignorant society now. We didn't even have to spike the punch bowl. We are lost, on the verge of a shooting war and involved in TV news discussions that I would never have thought belonged to national intercourse. I still can't get over the fact that a woman's pregnancy is not her own business. It should only be hers…ok, maybe her impregnator…or those she wants to inform…but no one else's. I grew up when it was nobody else's business but her own (maybe gossip on Ma Bell's party line). I fail to see why it is in the national discourse the way it is. Also, why do we announce on the news what our strategies are to help those poor people in Ukraine? Shouldn't what we're going to do be something the Russian leaders have to worry about? Why are we telling them?

Maybe the questions that used to belong to conceits of philosophy, poetry, the arts, have been lost to the information thumb, a tool in social engineering. Maybe the creator gave us a way out of the great question after all. We can now rely on technology to duplicate ourselves and not have to seek the larger question: why are we here? Meanwhile, anyway you look at it, we are a nation populated by scumbags with way too many firearms. What could go wrong?

SUBJECT: Re: Going, going, gone

William Burroughs wrote, "The public is going to take the place apart". He was a prophet. He was like family to us. We called him "uncle" and he was very generous. He gave me paintings and manuscripts. Burroughs had magnetic attraction you know. In the '50s, I found the book *Instantaneous Personal Magnetism* in an abandoned gold miner's shack near the Superstitious Mountains in Arizona. Burroughs had copy of it, too. "Already knew" was the attraction. He was always way ahead of the game.

Burroughs was one if my best friends, along with James Grauerholz. James calls my emails a "sewing circle" and sometimes feels he has to answer everyone, which he doesn't want to do. I'm getting to the age I have to jettison things, but I still have a copy of Jack Black's *You Can't Win*, Burroughs' first read, a book he turned me onto. It's the story of a man who made his way from Kansas City to the Northwest. His life marks the end of an era, the end of the frontier. Both William and I were familiar with the time, and the country, when that era was ending. Leonard Cohen had some songs in the Robert Altman film, *McCabe & Mrs. Miller*. Pam and the kids didn't like the movie because they couldn't figure out what it was about. It was like a documentary to me. I traveled through the Northwest in the '50s with my sister, who was a prostitute. She first married a lumber man in Oregon, got a divorce and then married Frank, the son of a Black madam and the Irish sheriff of Deadwood, South Dakota. Everybody liked old Frank, and he got me a job on the docks in San Francisco in the '60s.

SUBJECT: Fwd: Wild fire

The ancestors of the Hopi had to fight giants who wanted to eat them. That was in New Mexico, near Shiprock which is the stump of giant tree. I lived in Flagstaff, Arizona while I worked on the natural gas pipeline right of way to the California line. I sang: "Don't let the stars get in your eyes/ don't let the moon break your heart" on the way to work, in my 1952 Buick Roadmaster, the one I bought in Hollywood. I worked with my sister's husband who had a lumber mill in Prineville, Oregon which made finished molding. The Ponderosa was good for that. I also worked on a rock crusher in Crater Lake, where rock floated and the lumber sank. (Certain types, I forgot). I also worked with dynamite crew and rock drill on the Dalles Dam on the Columbia River. I bought a record player and had a Lionel Hampton LP with the "Rose Room" on it that I have never been able to find it again. I looked over San Francisco Bay from Twin Peaks, probably on Sandoz & Panama Red. I remember Alan Russo and I thought we were flying from there one time. I also worked on the Colorado River operating a D8 Caterpillar near Cibola, Arizona. Dad bought me a new 1952 GMC pickup when we lived in Blythe, California. He owned all the land along the interstate to Arizona line. I had a radio in the pickup and listened to the top pop songs, like, Johnny Ray's "Little White Cloud". I saw the cloud again today on the way to buy cat food, looking at the blue foothills of the Adirondacks. A giant hawk began following the car. I stopped to give it a peanut and some dry cat food, and told Pam it was carrying the soul of the kid who hit the sign behind us on his motorcycle. So much for experience and empiricism. Someone told me I'm 88 on Tuesday, and I suddenly felt it. I think my longevity has been a punishment for my sins when I can only sleep perchance to dream, then memories of my sins of lust and fast car tail fins invade my dreams.

SUBJECT: Re: Kansa

Kansa is my favorite word, I've always known it to mean "south wind", although according to Kip [WK Stratton], Kansa or Kanza or Kaanze is from a Siouan dialect and it means "south wind people" or sometimes just "wind people". He says in Oklahoma, the tribe is known as the Kaw and that the Bureau of Indian Affairs considers the Kaw to be part of the larger Sioux world. Kip also told me the Siouan dialect spoken by the Kaw, Dhegiha, is also foundational for the Osage, Quapaw, and Ponca languages, so it is possible that the Osage first applied the word "kaanze" to the Kaw. He said the word definitely would not have come from the Comanche, who speak a form of Aztec. There's a lot to Kansa, more than it may seem. The word "Kaw," by the way, seems to have come into use after people misread the abbreviation "Kan" on some handwritten French documents. There was an ad in the Garden City, Kansas paper for a minister at Plymell church. I was going to apply there as first agnostic preacher west of the Mississippi.

SUBJECT: How How How How Now Brown Cow

Ohyeah, I'm goin' back to wicthytitty and rebop the bebop blues and remember the kiddies, another Charlie P., an unknown teenager from Kansas City who played the Trocadero Club in Jay McShann's band, 50-cent cover after midnight. Even Satchmo shook up about his playin' whiffenpoofie. I'm going back to witchestitty and get me some Lifebuoy-clean chicks who know what it's for, good goodygirls who confess their sins, get born again and are ready to do it, not the cheap perfume of big city chicks who chippy around with no money down. We kept it square'cuz we liked it like that, not the crapolapolitical correct of newmoralitygodo today donchah know? Language first and then the culture. Aristotle knew that, too.

Some people in the South talked in metaphor to keep alive. I used to teach metaphor, not just simple comparison. I was just thinking of a word that became a denotative meaning from metaphor, and came up with "broadcasting", as in radio. They had to call it something: broadcasting, from the broadcasting of seeds. That was already in the language.

SUBJECT: Poetry questions

I've called myself a songwriter before, and now I'm a philosopher. Poet is a label that has connotations and denotations in our present civilization that I have left behind.

"Defined atoms", good. That idea was written about by Lucretius in his *De Rerum Natura*. Read the W.H.D. Rouse translation of that, from the Loeb Classical Library at Harvard. Rouse writes, "Lucretius was the inventor of the atomic theory: the most brilliant, and the most fruitful of all scientific hypotheses."

Ignorant poets over the last 2000 years ago have ruined that poem, especially more modern poets looking to make their own mark. Pitiful ignorance.

SUBJECT: Fools with Tools

I hate the bells. Hart Crane wrote about them in his poem, "The Idiot". Katherine Ann Porter lived with him at the time and she told me Hart was always trying to commit suicide. He was up on the roof of a hacienda one time when she told him, "Come on down, Hart. It isn't high enough and you'll only hurt yourself."

The Hunchback of Notre Dame rang the bells and said "beware of those with thin lips." Some newscasters get shots in lips to make theirs look puffy/fuller. Chuck Berry said, at concert in England, something about the blues, that the Brits say it differently. He said (paraphrase), "One has to have lips, like we do, to say it right", and then gave a demonstration: "B-B-Blues".

SUBJECT: No mo status quo

I might have to write an essay on tyranny, too. It's the latest fad now. The idiocy is spreading fast. Something causing it. No mo status qou. c

SUBJECT: Fw: Your Comment

I was petting my little kitty, Peaches, who has a bad eye. I have to get Peaches to a vet for a medical exam. She can't stay in the sunlight, so I thought up these poems.

JESUS IS MINE
For Patricia Elliott

It's Christmas time
I thought of a hymn about heavenly sunshine.
I didn't exchange gifts or cards this year
      only old saws
like, Buddy can you spare a dime?
      And old stories
when Bill was teaching you how to fly fish
      almost slipped into stream.
I should have stayed with you as planned
      in Lawrence and not
missed the road to St, Louie to meet up
      with Grant and Patti.
I pet my kitten under the sun rays and thought
of the arch of St. Louie, we're eating chop Suey.

(It's hell in New York.)

I sledded firewood in a blizzard yesterday.
Today I'm sitting in this pig sty of a room
might as well have a caul around my brain,
trying to write some thoughts.

We talk of "Uncle Bill"
who lay in the cold ground over that hill
probably snarling that death is a waste of time.

A stone-faced statue
of Chuck Berry born in the wind and carried in the
           rhythm of the winds
and the blues of a melancholy sunset over there.

He had his prize stolen, too
in the blind night of protest songs.
Boring as a painting of a landscape that
would make a better gift than the girl in
an ad on TV whistling for her boyfriend's present:
a new pickup truck ramming through the snow.
I have to get some firewood in the stove
and a last gasp of oxygen to get the flames arising!

NEW AGE MORALITY CLOCK

Of death gathers dust
on the Angel Flight of Fante
Dem tribe fems against old white males
can't say a word in freedom of speech
kids walk by with necks bent to iPhones
(they'll grow that way, future like clones)
inch worm directions in cars over a cliff
never learned landmarks, hills & streams.
I'll find my way home, reality is a dream.
Wanna be hipsters skinny legged britches
kissy kissy germs of prick teasing bitches
old age dying off at Church of The Unnoticed
new art of fat and food in chaos! Applause!
(Whatever happened to Brittany Spears? Who cares.)
Death is a waste of time.

SUBJECT: Re: Book covers

I still have the first book I read, *The Boxcar Children*. That book indeed embodies my philosophy that when great dreams don't happen, small treasures can still appear.

SUBJECT: Fw: Public School Nightmare

Our current national situation is the result of our national education system. I couldn't go to kindergarten in Yucaipa, California in 1939 because the state didn't have one. Instead, my sisters made me a "Yucaipa Valley Basement School" at our house. I remember everything from that time and was involved in "critical thinking", my sisters' argument of what color socks Bing Crosby's brother wore when he stopped in front of our house in his yellow Buick convertible.

I don't know, but the right-to-lifers must have the deep conscious idea that another little Jesus might be in there. But if Mary had an abortion, could we calculate how many lives would have been saved in wars, or how many wars can we assign to the Jesus religion? And if women ruled, would we have wars? I'm getting tired of seeing men killed on battlefields. Forever.

I saw on news the Orange Thing had top secret documents strewn all over the bed and the floor. He was probably laying on them, jerking off.

SUBJECT: Fwd: misery gentrified

And I think you are right about the city. We lived on the Bowery one year and when winter came the bums built barrel fires from pieces of pallets they got from trucks unloading to warehouses along the Soho streets. Now the grime and sweat and broken bottles have turned into art. I liked it better then, before gentrification.

SUBJECT: Re: Kansas rejects abortion amendment. The Wichita Eagle.

It's so ridiculous and ignorant that there is even a national discussion about something that is nobody's damn business but their own. I'd like to go back to Kansas to give a speech on abortion.

SUBJECT: Re: George Washington

I think I was teaching a special course at Johns Hopkins that year. The course was called "Words and Ideas". It could fulfill English101, for those smart enough to sign up and take it. Johns Hopkins was an all-male college then. I asked the guys what was their biggest concern was and they unanimously said, "getting an 'A' to keep out of Vietnam draft." Most of them were looking to continue studies in the medical profession, anyway. I said, "O.K. I don't like grades anyway." They all got their 'A'. It turns out it was a professor at Hopkins who started the cumbersome named course titled English Composition 101. Harvard then "stole" him and he made English Composition 101 the course to be followed by every college in the States, except for Elliott Coleman at Hopkins who invented the Johns Hopkins Writing Seminars to offer a course called "Words and Ideas", taught by the likes of someone he sent for, off the San Francisco docks.

Pam was working for *The Wall Street Journal* in D.C. when Reagan got shot. She saw the scene out her office window. I had to turn in my grades at George Washington and got "booted". My car had a medieval clamp on its wheel that prevented it from moving, for being in the loading zone. I had to go through the "Black experience" of city government and get over to Pam to raise a hundred bucks, cash, and go to City Hall, and then wait for the warden with the boot key to come by G.W. to free my car.

I've sometimes thought of listing places and courses I've taught, but I wouldn't know where to put them. The two poetry courses offered to me at American University interfered with my schedule at "The Cut", Jessup Prison. The prison population was 99% black. I tried to picture myself teaching poetry to privilege and realized I didn't have to teach the prison students the metaphor. Their language in life was metaphorical. Blues is a metaphor. In my first lecture I said that I was there to teach standard usage in writing, not to correct their vernacular. Those inmates were some of the best students I've ever had. I remember discussing the movie *The Burning Bed* with their class. The actress became the "welfare bitch" so my questions went like, "Mr. Johnson, where do you think the welfare bitch began to go wrong?"

Subject: Re: New Underground Comix and Rare Items Added

In some ways it's more difficult being 88 and seeing the changes in government that should not have been needed. Dad, in Kansas, invited the section gang of Mexicans working on railroad to our house to play music. Their kids were all bright eyed. They grew weed along the railroad tracks. As our "civilization" has developed, their children would have to go to a "home" for "rehabilitation" if they wanted to be part of society, and give up their lifestyle, their liberty and their pursuit of happiness.

Our message in the '50s was to stay cool and dodge the law, In the '60s, the charmers tried reason and intelligence, but it went nowhere. In the '70s, I taught a college writing course at The Cut, a 1930s structure between Baltimore & Washington, aka Jessup Prison. When I parked way away from the structure, I would hear a giant boom box of cacophony. I had to follow two guards into the bowels of the prison, guards who weren't armed because their weapons would have been taken away from them. Three floors of cells produced noise, spit and whatever flew through the air to the first floor. The sound never stopped until I got into the classroom. It was hell, the legal definition of "cruel and unusual punishment." Many of my students were in there for pot, for possession or selling. "Three strikes and you're out" stupid. Kamala Harris was at the Berkeley free speech rally in 1964, Harris in a stroller with her folks, when I and Allen Ginsberg and Neal Cassady went over. Three Rooms Press has published *Bad: The Biography of James Carr* that talks about life in San Quentin, where Neal was locked up from 1958 to 1960 for having two joints. I wrote a blurb for the book. I still wonder why the rest of the Beats didn't use their fame to help spring Neal.

P.S.: I get sick when I see New York State having to figure out where the money from legal pot sales will go. It makes me think of all the laws against freedom and happiness in this country. The Conservative Committee has just invited the Nazi from Hungary to speak. The Grand Old Party has become The Nationalist Christian Party. The fact that they are going to be in the Aryan minority has scared the shit out of them.

SUBJECT: Re: ASK THE DUST

My sister was an alcoholic, died on streets of San Francisco. Winos never liked being called "hopheads". There's a class distinction there. I finished Fante's book *Ask the Dust* last night. I wasn't into ethnicity/religions in my growing up, except for Mexicans on Kansas railroad, etc. Sammy had some good insights about the Aztec princess. I was in the LA basin in '39 eating oranges, like Fante, when it was still paradise. Big ripe navels, no longer available. I was back again in the '50s cruising Central Avenue, Black jazz clubs. Angel Flight was a relic then; they hadn't revived that yet. Bunker Hill in my 1950 Rocket 88. Fante had good imagery in his prose, better than Kerouac.

SUBJECT: Collage

When they say the 1950s were boring and Kansas was boring, I say that we kept it that way because we were cool and didn't want the squares to know anything, "like, what's happening". We were inventing own vernacular.

SUBJECT: split up in winter of death memories

Now I'm developing the bent-back-Cherry-Valley-walk, similar to Ezra Pound's line: "The enormous tragedy of a dream in the peasant's bent shoulders." My compassion has become my curse. I'm trying to clean up the house from last night's afterbirth pieces and I have to take out the dead kitten that the mommy cat brought me.

Subject: Re: Death is a waste of time

Shakespeare is essentially a pantheist like his influence, Lucretius, who sees everything around him as holy, just as everyone who calls themselves an "artist" should. As my authority, Rouse, would have it: "When I count the clock and see bright day sink into night, when I behold the violet withering or dark curls streaked with silver, when I see the trees stripped of their leaves, which early sheltered the herd from the heat, and summers green corn girded up in sheaves and borne to the wagon white and bearded, then, thinking of you, I fear that you must go along with time's waste, since all lovely things die as fast as they see others grow to take their place. Then there is no difference against time save to breed, against the day when you are taken away."

Take that shit.

PART HISTORY

SUBJECT: Sunset of the Heart

I found a minute this morning, from taking care of things, to write this, after watching the news last night. Let me know if you spot anything wrong in it.

> SUNSET OF THE HEART
> Elegy for Tyre Nichols
>
> I knew you only through the media
> the one that brings us murders, killings, mass shootings, wars
> in some continuous evil of state armed and dangerous
>   (sometimes disguised).
>
> It happened in the days of old Jerusalem, in Dallas and
>   once before in Memphis too.
> Good souls that only want such things in life as
>   beauty in the setting sun
> are always hunted by mankind's evil.
>
> I don't know why Good Souls are hunted, chased down,
> crucified, beaten, shot in the back, or snipers of state disguised
> and wars that in the brains of men contain an evil in this world.
>
> Your call for "Mom" is heard around the world of Good Souls
> calling out an echo of consciousness in whispering wind
> of beautiful sunsets that I will call Tyre Nichols Sunsets.

SUBJECT: History out of the blue

Time for calls out of the blue…I got a call from a Moe Armstrong who lived with Stella Levy, Peter Orlovsky and my old girlfriend, Ann Buchanan. She's in one of those photos in front of City Lights. Moe's pad was on Laguna, around from Oak Street in the Haight. I thought Stella had passed but she's still with us. Moe is in New Haven now with cancer from Agent Orange. He had gone to Santa Fe from San Francisco to live for a while. Lots of space out there for spirits to come and go.

The photo in front of City Lights is from while we were living at 1403 Gough Street. Years later, Pam and I lived around the corner, on Post Street, where we had the old multilith we printed ZAP on and had nude parties, which were in vogue then. Ann must have taken those photos, as she is in other ones taken at the same time. She wasn't my wife, though we were on the road to common law. She "jumped ship" in NYC and took up with Warhol bunch at The Factory. Gerard Malanga, my close friend, said he "fell head over heels in love with her." There is a link on Google of Andy Warhol's Screen Test, the 13 Most Beautiful Women. Ann is first one on that.

From Pam: I was not with Charley when he was living on Gough St. The first place we lived in together was a Tenderloin Hotel, bathroom down the hall. Then, we shared an apartment with Betty, his sister, and Frank, her husband. It was on the hill above Market Street. See *Last of the Mocassins* for more on that. Next, we got an apartment on Nob Hill, one of the trolley streets. It had a Murphy bed. After that, we left for Wichita with Roxie Powell, Maggie Harms and her daughter, Maia. As usual, I was sick as a dog in the mountains. When we got to Wichita, Charley showed off his skateboarding skills to his nieces and managed to break his ankle. He had an operation that put a pin in the ankle. I had to read for Charley at WSU, Jim Meacham had scheduled a paid reading there. I didn't read again for 30 years. I went on to NYC while Charley recuperated. I returned when Ginsberg visited Wichita. Charley picked me up at the airport and he left for Lincoln with Allen. Later on, we went to Lawrence. That's also in *Last of the Mocassins*. We left in late Spring for San Francisco, along with a few friends, in a car that broke down in Garden City and couldn't be repaired. We took a bus to Denver and stayed with Wayne Sourbeer for a few days until money arrived. Charley got mugged walking to Gough Street once. They stole a book he was carrying for Glenn Todd. Glenn found us the Post Street apartment. It had been a dance studio. The rest is history. We stayed a couple of months at Gough Street during the summer of '68, in Maggie Harms' apartment. There's also more on that in *Last of the Mocassins*. P.S.: Charley has no sense of dates or time.

I don't know if Eric Baizer is still around or not. Last I heard, he went to LA. He bet me ten bucks he could write a press release that would appear in *The Washington Post*. He wrote a release as a joke and it appeared in the *Post*, in the "Washington Talk" column, as well as in *The New York Times*, about me heading up "Poets For Reagan" when Ronnie came to power. The poetry liberals went crazy and I became the enemy. I was also interviewed by Michael M. Mooney for his book, *The Ministry of Culture*. The academic poets took what we had to say seriously because their fellowships and grants might be jeopardized. The whole industry was upset. After that came out, parents complained that they paid big bucks for their kids to get in MFA programs for no apparent monetary reward. The money was already spoken for. *Poets & Writers* and other organizations came to the rescue, using poetry as social engineering, a sleight of hand, stuff that lasts today in there being unknown poets at the inaugurals. We took Ginsberg to the NEA and he got himself and Peter and everyone he knew fellowships, while pamphleteering for his school. Everyone got a fellowship except me. Ginsberg ended up getting the CIA to fund his Buddhist master's university, Naropa in Boulder, Colorado, complete with it being able to give college credits. It all became a piece of trumpishpootin propaganda, using poetry as the shell. The Fed money that was given out was based "only on quality", and the poets who determined quality were select friends of friends, who awarded the money to friends. Sound familiar?

SUBJECT: Re: 100 years of Jack Kerouac

I realized what a bore Kerouac was when I found myself sitting between him and Allen at a NYC bar, after taping the William F. Buckley show, the one with Ed Sanders. Kerouac joins the over-rated assholes of *New York Times* paper-famers, the billionaire financiers, the Bobby Dylans, the Andy Warhols, et al, the boring people their writers can't stop writing about. It's a moot point now, the world teetering on its apocalypse. Kerouac couldn't drive a stick shift. I was on the road when his mommy was washing his diapers.

Kerouac was the establishment! A good Republican east coast boy, like thousands of others wanting to get away from their mama, going out for competitive sports. He thought when hipster Herbert Huncke used the word "beat", that it was related to "beatitude" or some shit. Kerouac could have used his fame to try to get Neal out of San Quentin, when Neal was in for two joints. He never did. Neal's wife, who Kerouac was balling, thought it was a good idea that Neal go to prison to teach him not to be a bad boy. Total ignorance. BTW, ignorant New York State doesn't know how to distribute weed or how to distribute the money that it'll make from selling it. This, after 100 years of torturing mostly black/brown men in maximum security prisons, for selling weed, for having weed. The nation of the established ignorance and the education system that Kerouac lived in gives us the ignorant Repub(erty) nation of today. Who reads this Kerouac-as-hero shit? Who cares what the stock market is doing? Makes my ass wanna dip snuff.

SUBJECT: Re: lizard brain

I don't know where I put my pot. That's the trouble with geriatrics smoking that stuff.

Unfortunately, the Pootin freak can point to Bush who shocked and awed an invasion of sovereign nation and killed its leader under a false premise. Each of our invasions, and the lies told by Cheney, McNamara, Rumsfeld, et. al, has killed many innocent people and continues to do so.

Hitler's motto, "A lie repeated often enough becomes the truth", has now taken over the party of "Tear down that wall" Reagan and Ike, who felt sorry for Russian losses and gave them the wall in the first place. Humanity is trying to raise its head again with Ukraine. We can see now why Putin and Trump are blood brothers. Dangerous situation having nukes in the hands of Hitler-like mentality.

SUBJECT: Re: Fw: Mail call

Mike, you'll go past the Chalk Pyramids and the Eye of the Needle where Billy (my son, who turned me onto your music) and I heard the voice of the Game Lord. Ike lived in Abilene. His pop was dairy milker. The Uppities who lived across tracks looked down on them because they lived on other side where the Texican trail riders hung out. Bob Dole lived nearer the Colorado border. It would be good to have Republicans like that around again, but we don't and may never have that again. Billy and I didn't go to caves around Louisville because I was still recovering from flu and a little drink of medicine William Burroughs gave me in Lawrence. He promised, "It will kick in on the other side of Kansas City," which it did. I slept while Billy drove. Pretty soon you'll have more miles under your belt than I do! P.S.: Billy and I were on our way back from Missoula where he was in college. Billy insisted against my advice that I stay his dorm room. That's where I caught the flu. I told Billy to talk to Burroughs about Missoula and Burroughs told us how his father used to take him fishing in the rivers up there. I'll be 87 this month and I remember what Kay Boyle said once to me when I was working at San Francisco State: "At my age, don't talk about yourself, even when asked."

I told the interviewer from Greece that maybe technology is designed to erase the "why" in our brains so that we can just click on and on. The iPhone is creating an evolutionary change, bent necks and bigger thumbs, so we can forget the big question. I thought the interview was supposed to be about music, "those dying generations at their song." I must have scared him off. Yeats must have been reading Kant's philosophy in writing "Sailing to Byzantium", the form of the heavens, the "Grecian goldsmiths", etc. Meanwhile, in this country, the "pole in the hole" is still the challenge. Aristophanes was probably right in his "Clouds", there are no answers and we are crazy. Look as us now, a pregnant woman's future is in the high clown court. We've become a dumbed-down nation, with the "greatest army" crashing battleships and billion-dollar stealth fighters that tried to land on carrier they weren't supposed to land on, blah-blah shit storm. The check-out guy at the grocery store said, "Yeah, we've gone nuts, electing a cult leader who likes gold toilets seats." Howl at the moon is all that's left. Another time riding with Dad on the prairie, we watched a calf kick up its legs, and he said, "Everything wants to live, and shows it."

Ezra Pound's politics were always a thing. He said he was trying to prevent World War Two. I had a copy of his speeches titled "Roosevelt and the cause of World War Two" (or something like that) that I showed to Lawrence Ferlinghetti, or maybe Larry had it, I can't remember. Pound's *Cantos* seemed difficult to most people, but hip scholar Branaman used to read them to me at night, high on bennies, clubbing in the '50s. Pound said the cantos were like people sitting around talking, kind of a historical cut-up, I guess. Ginsberg wanted me to go to Spoleto with him to meet Pound. I was working and now wish I had gone. Allen brought back tapes with, as I remember, Pound saying his radio broadcasts were silly, or something like that. This was after Pound had served time in prison/nut house. The "Usura" Pound raved about was clearly Italian and an aspect of his adopted country. Italy has a history of it, from Caesar, who charged 100% interest, to the modern-day mobsters. Pound's daughter, Mary de Rachelwitz, was in touch with me when she was in New York and invited me to Hailey, Idaho for a Pound celebration. She said Robert Creeley and Lawrence Ferlinghetti were invited, so I figured all the wind would be sucked out. Mary dismissed the radio broadcasts as an embarrassment and sort of nutty. I'm no scholar/authority on Pound's life/work or his politics. There's probably reason in his thinking somewhere, but who knows. Economics is a crazy field anyway.

SUBJECT: Re: cars

The pre-war hydra-matics were sloppy but they got beefed up during the war. I have a picture of my 1950 Olds 88 convertible somewhere. I used to drag race it at stop lights by putting one foot on the brake and one on the gas pedal until the nose raised in the air. When the light changed, I let off the brake and floorboarded it. It took off like the rocket it was named after. I drove with another bennie head to his "old folks at home/ ace in the hole" trailer outside Bakersfield. He knew where the bar was in Oildale, where young Merle Haggard played. Merle grew up living in a boxcar, roughnecks from the oil fields all around. I worked a while at the train yards in Wichita. It was a good job and the boxcars were well made, a home for anyone. I'd like to have one now. Lyin' Dick Cheney beat hobos off the trains and probably shot them, too. I'm glad his daughter has a brain.

SUBJECT: Huncke's Words

I saw a special on Roy Orbison the other night. Sam Phillips at Sun Records dismissed him as a balladeer when Orbison recorded there with Elvis Presley and Charley Feathers early on, before any of them were known. Orbison was unique. It is Hank Williams, not Hank Williams, Senior as Shelton (Hank 3) duly corrected me. He said, "There was only one Hank Williams." Shelton hates commercial country, too. The stuff propagated by his father and Johnny Cash, who were trying to sound like George Jones. George's "He Stopped Loving Her Today" is one of the all-time great country songs. Hank Williams, George Jones and Bill Monroe are my trinity, with a lot of close seconds. Like, Jimmy Rogers, the father of country music, and Woody Guthrie, the dust bowl home boy. I grew up listening to my mother play their tunes. Peter Orlovsky was the only Beat I knew into country. He was a good yodeler.

I didn't get into poetry until after military school, after dropping out and traveling, and then going back to Wichita U., except for my poem at age four, on our way to California on Route 66 in a wheat truck: vacha peecha vocha peecha/vocha peecha voo/hip hip hooray/the dogs are coming. I don't know if any the Beats shared my love for Hank Williams, but they say Charley Parker annoyed his jazz colleagues by playing Hank Williams on juke boxes everywhere they went.

I prefer Rod McKuen's poetry to Ginsberg's, who said I had an old-fashioned modesty. Rod named me as influence to him with a list of greats, which was an honor. I'm still trying to find a book he dedicated to me and gave me at the B.B. King Club in Times Square. I never figured out why those children flipped over the word "beat". Like Huncke said, it was a common expression among the hip. In the '50s, I would have pegged most of the Beats as squares. You know I think Kerouac was over-rated. I loved Burroughs. He was family and claimed he never considered himself a beat anyway. Allen was too complicated. It would take a book to explain how complicated. He told me at his folks' house that he brought a black girl home and his folks kicked them out, and that's why he turned homo. I'd never heard that before, and don't know if it was true. Ginsberg was like the Orange Thing in some ways. He had a hard time with the truth and was real good at manipulation. Ray Bremser was a true beat.

Laki Vazakas sent me Huncke's words, from an interview they did: "Fuck Allen, he tells me I'm no longer a Beat. He said there are only three of us who are really Beats. I thought he was gonna say me right away, like a chump. And I said, 'Well, who is that?' And he said, 'Burroughs, myself and Kerouac.' I don't know why they use the expression because I meant it in a weary, beat way. There was nothing beatific about it, I can tell you that. When I say I'm beat, I'm beat. I'm beat to the socks, or I don't have any money, or I'm tired and I need some rest. I'm just beat. And that's exactly what I meant."

SUBJECT: Good news

We haven't had a fightin' Dem since LBJ. Nixon peeled off the hardhats who didn't like barefoot hippies. Clinton finished off the unions with NAFTA. Where were the Democrats during the Kellogg strike? Bernie showed up. The middle class has dissolved into an educated professional class and into a large minimum wage Lite Beer class that's prone to celebrity worship. This country's been convulsing since 11/22/63.

I used to think my ideas would have to be kept secret from society, like Kafka wanted his. No time for ideas now. I can hardly get anything done and I haven't had a rational thought in years.

SUBJECT: Re: Re:

I'm a Western person. Dad was born in Indian Territory, before Oklahoma became a state. President Cleveland gave my granddad some land in Palo Apache country for his stagecoach run. Google Plymell, Kansas and see the subsidized corn silos, silos holding corn for gasoline, that make the place look like a moonscape instead of a prairie. I'm on no other social media, so I use email. I only know to forward and reply.

I saw on TV that eastern investors are buying up water rights in Cibola, Arizona, that it's become a gated riverfront community. Dad and I used to clear brush there along Colorado River when only two people lived there, a brother and sister, who lived in a dirt floor shack and who invited us in to eat wild burro. A pile of hooves outside, along with the sidewinders, a kind of rattlesnake they also ate. There were scorpions and Gila monsters there that I don't think they ate. Once a guy helping me to lift a piece of metal was touched by scorpion, not stung, just touched, and he said he felt ice cold. Dad and I almost perished in Cibola by not having enough water. We saw buzzards circling over a body that didn't make it from Mexico. That was a common sight. We made it to a "cool can" on a tractor that had a little hot water left in it. There wasn't a real road to Cibola. I used to take a tractor out to smooth the trail. I drove my first semi-truck down there, to haul a bulldozer. Dad later bought me a brand new 1952 GMC pickup when we lived in Blythe, with a radio I turned on to hear Johnny Ray, whose songs were at the top of the Billboard charts. I lied about my age (you were supposed to be 18) and got a job on pipeline that went past an abandoned gold miner's shack near Superstitious Mountain. I found a book there, *Instantaneous Personal Magnetism*, which I later gave to William Burroughs. He'd already read it. Burroughs had land out west, near Pharr, Texas and was growing pot down there in the late '40s, with Herbert Huncke, and later on, Allen Ginsberg and Neal Cassady. After a while, Cassady had to convince Allen to leave, he'd become too annoying, too clingy. Burroughs, Cassady and Huncke drove a Jeep full of weed, from Pharr to New York. It wasn't much good and only got $100 for it.

Dad had an eye for the future but couldn't keep things. I could have been a multi-millionaire now, a house on the riverfront and millions more in water rights. Water is more precious than oil in the West. The same goes with our family farm, below Plymell, Kansas. It's the best wheat land, and the best oil and gas land. It made the Mennonites multi-millionaires. They're the ones who bought our land. Mom took the wheat truck out to them to gather scrap metal during World War Two, but they wouldn't give to the war effort. Anyway, I guess I can't hold on to things either. I "gave away" some of the best properties in Cherry Valley, eight of them, and, if I hadn't, I could be worth more than a million. I'm selling out this summer. I need a warmer climate in winter.

Allen said my writing wasn't good enough for the National Endowments of the Arts to award me monies, even with all their grants, panels and prizes. I wonder about his? Pam and I took Allen to meet the c'suckers at the NEA. They got so exited they gave Allen, and his friends, the store. After all, we lived in a better house than Allen did.

SUBJECT: Re: How's your face

We are all suffering from the evil of greed, of some kind, every day. It's baked in the American consciousness. Maybe there'll be no capitalistic democracy next. People aren't people anymore. They are likenesses on TV. They are more video than flesh. That's why people shoot people without a reason.

The Democrats have turned dumb again. Emerson foresaw what was to be, the Republicans working the system better, smarter. That's given us the orange menace that's overtaken us. In the '80s with coke money and derivatives the government was deep in criminality, too. They were encouraging farmers to take on more land until they went broke and didn't know it. There was a documentary about a farmer who didn't know what happened until they came for his new machinery. There was an article years ago in the Atlantic about the milk industry which concluded the government kept it so puzzling no one could ever understand it. No one knows exactly what a quart of milk would cost from cow to store. When I was teaching at University of Maryland, a guy from the farm program took a faculty job, came to teach. I asked him why he gave up a higher paying job in the government, and he said the farm program and its subsidies was kept as a monster that no one could understand. He said a good idea could never make it. Ideally, a dictatorship is appealing, simple, but there's never been a benevolent dictator. Democracy has proved to be a beacon, a hope, but messy to apply.

I wanted Elizabeth Warren, Bernie Sanders, Stacy Abrams, people with smarts and gusto. I distrust the tired old machine of "good guys in government". We are in a dark winter. History is buried quickly. We saw a guy coming out of grocery store with red t-shirt, the orange guy's name in big letters and "the tour of revenge" written underneath. Sick. A gun waiting in his car, no doubt, just itching for an altercation.

I went to military school in San Antonio for my one and only year of high school. We watched President Truman fire General MacArthur, because MacArthur wanted to take his army across the parallel, which might have been a good idea after all. Cadet officers would inspect sleeping quarters and they'd have first-year venerable cadets, like those from South America, who didn't know the customs/language, go down on them. No one has figured out sex and power either. "The oppressor's wrong, the proud man's contumely, the pangs of despis'd love, the law's delay, the insolence of office, and the spurns, that patient merit of the unworthy takes..."

I have a gender/sex/politics essay in me but I'm afraid to write it. I was making a point to Glenn Horowitz (who has bought some of my rarities, handled Dylan's archives, etc.) that "woman" is so desired that most jokes, plays, innuendos, etc. invoke her. His wife, a Buddhist feminist, took it wrong and got angry. We should look back to Aristophanes, who thought male/female were at one time the same, and then broke apart. Anyway, as an empiricist, and learning mostly by experience, I would need a woman to help me write this. Anne Waldman told me that at Naropa she and Allen Ginsberg sat cross-legged and masturbated together while looking at each other naked.

Subject: Re: the hippies called it karma

We are seeing the product of an educashun system that got dumbed-down generation two decades ago. It's worse than liberals of right and left coast can comprehend. They're out of touch, like the enlightened citizens of Germany, who were sophisticated enough to listen to Brahms and Wagner, but didn't know enough to say anything during the rise of brownshirts. The gunsgod put him in power and the Third Reich is here...now. Burroughs claimed everyone who owns a frying pan owns death. Everyone who own a gun owns death. It's much easier to exhibit the power, to act as the creator, when we can't comprehend why we are here...it's easier just to snuff it. The pathological anxiety of the "undiscovered country from whose bourn no traveler returns" has finally overcome the human mind, and no longer just puzzles the will. I gave up packing my .45 on the Arizona desert in the '50s, when I saw a pitiful "wetback", on a thousand-mile hike wearing homemade huaraches with scrap-tire tread soles, look at me, wondering if I was going to shoot him.

You are on Native Land. A sacred place. Remember that. Take a hike while you still can.

Subject: Re: "scarfing" not in my spell check

I got lost in a dream riding in a new Chevy, beating drums on the dashboard, high on bennies and boo, going to the next club to hear sax wailing. When the car radio found a good station, it was high beams on, driving to Joplin, Missouri in my Pontiac, Hank Ballard and The Midnighters on. And down Corpus Christi way, on the beach, that South Texas station was good. Long John Hunter first heard B.B. King on that, went and saw B.B play, and ended up leaving his mule and plow to play the Lobby Club in Juarez. Janis Joplin heard that station, too.

Innocent times in Wichita, we thought so groovy, finishing the clubs at 3 a.m. and going to the original White Castle. Hustling punch board games in beer joints for gas money on the way to Kansas City on the thruway, past where Bird was born, down near the tracks in Kansas City, Kansas. Cars had cloth seats, maybe mohair, sometimes leather, and smelled better than the vinyl today. "To score" would be a "J" or criss-cross bennies or scarfing box in the back seat. "Scarf your box" was the vernacular of the '50s, By the '60s, it was "eat your pussy". Post-war years, the greatest. I had a new 1951 Chevy with fender skirts and leaded gas. I tried to go to my sophomore year of high school in Wichita. Huh-uh, man, no way. Gas was 15 cents a gallon, I could lie about my age and get a job down the line any old time. High school in the rear view. Go man, go drop out. Innocent times. Time was tight, anything you did was right. I saw Nicca's dad's movie, *Rebel Without a Cause*, about five times when it came out. Goodnight, sweetheart, I'm petting my cat who knows where it's at.

Subject: Re: Quote translated

I just had a conversation about translations with a friend, who quoted Jorge Luis Borges as saying, "The original is unfaithful to the translation". James Grauerholz told me Borges really said, "Una traducción está como una mujer. Si estuve bonita, no estabía fidel. Si estuve fidel, no estabía bonita." That's: "A translation is like a woman. If she is beautiful, she is not faithful. If she is faithful, she is not beautiful."

I got a note from the French translators of *Last of the Moccasins* wondering what I meant when I wrote, "that thing that chokes itself out of greed and gear." Well, I told them they could retranslate it as greed and gadgets, that it will never lose its meaning, but then we both realized it was a typo, that the f and g are next to each other. They build nations now with greed and guns. In the Risorgimento, they used grammar and poetry to forge a nation.

It was the *The Freewheelin' Bob Dylan* LP I played for Ginzy at Gough Street, in San Francisco. "Blowin' in the Wind" is on it. I remember Allen puzzling if he should like an Okie imitation, Woody accent or not. Dylan had just been booed off stage in Hollywood. After Dylan got famous, Allen would play nothing but Dylan on the tape recorder/boom box that Dylan gave him. He had that in the VW bus he bought with his Gugenheim money, that's what we drove across Kansas in. I told him not to play that shit around me. Allen was caught up in hippie shit at the time.

Neal Cassady was always cussing out Jack Kerouac, who couldn't drive a stick shift without grinding gears or ruining clutch. People are not taught to drive stick anymore. I wrote *Last of the Mocassins* for my Johns Hopkins thesis and sent it to Larry Ferlinghetti and he published it as was, without corrections, in 1970. Johns Hopkins gave me a Masters' Degree if I would come there and teach a course in writing. I left a good job on the docks in San Francisco to do so. Pam's mother corrected some of *Last of the Mocassins* after Ferlinghetti published it.

Subject: Re: The Book

"The Arts" are now and have always been a social engineering tool for government to keep women and minorities in place. Better to have them in arts and crafts, and keep control of their bodies. Prizes and grants are like Orwellian tools. It's difficult in this environment for the public to discerned the merits of each artist. "The book" might be worth a lecture, but a book about books? You did more with that email book of mine to keep the form "new", like what Mike Watt is doing with my "opera". Does it meet the Pound dictum of "poetry is news that stays news"? Maybe, maybe not.

SUBJECT: Re: In answer to today's news about the "Wall"

In the '50s, my dad had some land and a farmhouse outside of Yuma, Arizona. He leased his land to a grower and lived in the house. Onetime, a "wetback" came to the door. He had on homemade huaraches made from leather attached through holes in a piece of tire tread. He said he was hungry and could work. My dad spoke a little Spanish, and explained he didn't have any work but he gave him some money for groceries and said there was a store about a half mile down the road where he could buy food. My dad thought that was the end of it, but a few weeks later, that Mexican man came to the door and insisted on paying back the money. Another time, I was carrying a World War Two .45 pistol out on the desert, shooting up cactus as a stupid kid would. I saw another figure walking up from the river. He studied me, obviously concerned that I was armed. I put the .45 back in holster and went the other way, somewhat ashamed that I put someone who had been struggling to keep alive for hundreds of miles in added fear. There is no justice. Man is a bad hombre. Sometimes there is an individual instance of good and evil, but what's written is not always reality. Tear down that wall!

Our neighbor across the street blowing her driveway and lawn clean with her noisy high-pollute gas engine blower is doing more damage than she does with her car. She doesn't realize she is contributing double to climate change. Big industry cashes in on the dumb. Get that stray leaf off my lawn! Humans are done for.

Yeah, the American DNA no longer has something to unite us. The karmavirus canceled it. I always liked old Mehico anyway. Last time I was down there, they still had Model T taxi cabs. I gave my friend Mexican Benzedrine and he drove all the way from Guadalajara talking to himself. If you see something good, I might come down there. "If you see Rosemary, tell her I'm comin' home to stay." If you don't know who sang that, you're a square! Viva Zapata!

SUBJECT: Re: Gregory Corso Biography

Sorry, I don't have time for this literary stuff anymore. A great Fourth? If you call getting down with Dana Bash, watching CNN and second-rate entertainment, while the country shoots up over 10 million dollars in fireworks that could have gone to starving people and animals "great". Maybe this annual misconception will keep the shooters and meth-head insurrectionists at bay for another year. I thought it mostly ignorant but will admit that Pam and I and Elizabeth sat on the mall in D.C. years ago and watched millions of dollars (mostly mob money) go up in fireworks. Tonight's music made me ill, if anything. Billy Ray Cyrus could use a shave and haircut (and a bath and a better voice).

SUBJECT: Re: Annie Ross and Count Basie

Yeah, this is it! This is 100% hip! The nathen shaken nowhere little muthafuckers today with backward hats shading sun from their eyes with one hand, the other thumbing a gadget, wonder whut's happenin in infonothing universe. They say nothing was happening in post-war '50s except Thanksgiving dinner and football games. Maybe for the likes of Kerouac and Ginsberg, but I was high on boo and bennies. I remember greeting "Mister Basie" going into Orpheum Theater in Wichita. I was polite, not trying to be hip because he would know. He smiled and responded politely. There was none of this "political correct" shit that got the Goon elected. I hope you watched the next video, when Big Joe Williams comes out and Annie displays her "axevox". Hip was always integrated; music was the family. There was no hate speech because no one cared about unhip hate in the other universe. Jazz ate the word jellybeans. You should try to find Joe William's version of "Goin' to Chicago"… "I'm tired of your NY joy/I'm going back to Illinois…Goin' to Chicago/Sorry, but I can't take you/Ain't nuthin' in Chicago/a monkey woman like you can do."

I have the Annie Ross/King Pleasure LP with Annie singing "Twisted", "Farmer's Market", et al. I retrieved it from a trash bag some newbie hippie threw out in San Francisco, up near Larry's pad on Potrero Hill. He said he was headed to the Head Shop to hear Ravi Shankar, the Lawrence

Welk of India. I last saw Annie some years ago in a little club in D.C. She was catching a plane back to Ireland. No jazz was happening here in the States...all gone.

If it wasn't bad enough that I turned Ginsberg onto Dylan's music to then have Dylan become a poet and steal my nowhere muthafuckernobel! Ginsberg turned the mommydaddy beat & squarebabyboomers on to the likes of Johnny Cash, who lived in his casket dressed in black. The squarebabies thought Cash was the greatest country singer. He did some good things, but I saw him as 40% phony, like his pal Dylan was 40% poet. Cash's music leads to Barph Grooks, er, Garth Brooks and chicken shit commercial country.

This country is now left with government poets and artists, "subsidized lint" as the great Carl Weissner called it. And academics grind out cookbook chapbooks while our society comes apart and no one seems hip to the police murderers shooting black people in the old "drop the knife" lie routine. I was at the peace march in Berkeley where Kamala Harris folks' brought her in baby carriage. I wrote in a poem during the Vietnam War: "Where were you before a protest was needed?" After illegal wars and the invasion of sovereign countries, like the land we stole from the Indians, our country itself has become illegal. Mobster movies won Oscars. We loved them. We got one. He's our leader and Commander-in-Chief. Did you watch the prophetic movie *Idiocracy*? We are there.

Too late for advice. After this, I'm through with the arts. Never meant for me. Human intercourse has turned to babble. Evil feeds it into the consciousness to block good action. More people with guns will kill more people. A fresh drop of blood appeared just now out of nowhere. A little bigger than those you see on foreheads. I consider it a sign.

SUBJECT: Re: They don't teach that in driving classes

My dad always made me keep a firm grip on steering wheel of our trucks. Those were made of carbon then, not plastic, which is what's produced now. The seats were always made of cowhide. The radio in my '49 Caddy had an automatic selector, which was hot stuff in those days. The hand selector knob is still the best. It's o.k. on a long stretch to take one hand off wheel to find a radio station. Of course, our trucks didn't have radio and my dad wouldn't even have a heater because it cost extra. It would have been nice to have in the Dakotas.

I'm thinking of selling my Subaru because it has too many distractions. It started talking to me and I had to pull over and shut it off because I didn't know what I pressed. Also, that damn TV thing on dash had a green line crawling across it. I had just put in "Rocket 88" by Jackie Brenston to check out the cd player. One of the YouTube videos for that song has a picture of my 1950 Olds 88 convertible in it. I asked Pam what was the line crawling across the dash TV. She thought it indicated how much volume. I said that would only help if I was deaf and if I was deaf, I wouldn't be listening to a cd anyway. Who the hell wants to be distracted looking at a green line on the dash?

Everyone knew if you left the radio on in old cars, you would run the battery down. The first time I left the keys in the Subaru, it ran the battery down. It talks to you about everything else, but not a peep on that. Big words display all the time on the dash: PASSENGER SEAT BELT IS ON. There's no one sitting there. Why the hell do I care?

SUBJECT: Funny Facebook censor

Like Burroughs' father said: I had a dog named Rover, when he died, he was dead all over.

SUBJECT: The Trashing of America. A revised edition?

It would have to be re-designed, of course, with new graphics. I never knew why John Giorno put that Nixon thing on the back cover. That was a good collage at the back, but Lita Hornick kept that so it probably can't be reprinted very well. The photos were taken by Ted Manovitch, a rather temperamental guy Maureen Owen brought up here. I couldn't get him to take a photo of Burroughs at our dinner table. I like Les Levine's front cover, but it isn't necessary. I'd like to keep the credits to the other publications.

It's a good record of where those poems appeared and it can be updated, probably. Could probably I use S. Clay's inscribed Checkered Demon as the frontispiece? Maybe those first lines of Allen's "Alone" poem he gave me when writing I was writing "Glory Revolution" could be substituted for the opening stanza there? Maybe include mine and Burroughs' collaboration? That was before he met James. A kid found those two pages and Allen's typescript of the poem he gave me, and everything I was printing then, in pizza boxes under Leland Meyerzove's bed after he died. He had copped. I don't know if all that would be too complicated for a "revised edition".

Whatever Bill Roberts wants to do is always fine with me. John Giorno put that book together while living at the old Y, across the hall from what later became Burroughs' bunker. I didn't know the cover artist, Les Levine, personally. He was a friend of Giorno's. I went to Lita Hornick's parties on Fifth Avenue. She had guards in her apartment protecting the Warhols. She had book party for me upstairs at Gotham, where the famous poets used to have had parties. Mine was last one, I think, before it closed down. Unfortunately, she took us to an expensive restaurant where Mary and Claude, and another Frenchman of the Situationist Party in France and his wife, tagged along and used racial slurs as Frenchmen do. I repeated them at table, in front of Lita and her husband. She said if I wasn't a great poet, she'd have me thrown out, and that she hadn't had that kind of thing happen since an incident with LeRoi Jones. I was very sorry because I liked her even though her Kultur books were sloppy printed, only a $500 advance, no royalties, like Ferlinghetti. She was good friend of Gerard Malanga's, who probably got wind of the restaurant scene. I saw Gerard's autographed copy of *The Trashing of America* on eBay one time.

SUBJECT: Re: Send it around if you want

SO LONG LARRY, BIG SALUTE TO THE ANGELS OF THE GREATEST GENERATION. SAY HELLO TO NEAL & EVERBODY. SEE YA SOON, CHARLEY PLYMELL

Coincidence, speaking of God, a Jehovah Witness just called. I told him I'm agnostic. A in Latin is "no" and gnostic is "to know". I said, "I don't know. You claim to know. Don't call me again," and hung up.

To remind you, I was the one who took Ginsberg to the National Endowment for the Arts and introduced him to a round of literary cocksuckers headed by Len Randolph, who later appointed Peter Coyote as something or other. I was one of the first to recognize the NEA scams, they play out like Trumpism, appointing suck asses, making up rules to suit their interests and having a committee of peers decide what is "quality". I always believed that 300 grand (or more) was a big sum to throw at one poet, "quality" or not. Like A.D., I no longer care for the label of "poet". It has no meaning anymore. Boy scouts, like Gary Snyder, and this latest generation of academic poets, have made the label meaningless. Scratch a poet and find a Trumpster. A cowboy saying, from when I was riding in the rodeo: "Makes my ass wanna dip snuff."

We were called "punks" in the '50s mainly because of our duck-ass haircuts and faux-suit-style clothes. We were "different", that's all it took in Wichita. Punk, of course, had a gay insinuation, though most of the male population in Wichita was gay, although that word didn't have today's connotation. The definition seemed to be that males, from oil field workers to cars dealers, were not considered gay if they had their cocks sucked by another guy. I went out for football the beginning of my second year of high school at North High in Wichita, after having completed my first year at a military school in San Antonio. The coach would make insinuating remarks if we couldn't do the push-ups, saying things, like, next we'd be sitting to piss. I said fuck it to school, and peeled across the high school lawn in my brand new '51 Chevrolet and never looked back.

SUBJECT: Re: Garden of Eden is in Kansas

As an addendum to the Garden of Eden discussion below, I was just thinking watching the Mars landing that whatever is in charge of human existence might permit us to re-create ourselves and solve the problem, the idea, of not being here. There is a lot of "existential" anxiety just being aware of living. That word gets thrown around a lot now, "existentialism", but if we remake ourselves through electronics, robots, etc. maybe we can leave out the big question. After all, it has taken the church over 2000 years to get people to believe in virgin birth, even forming councils to make it "official". The big political lie is not too hard to imagine. We tend to go to war over lies, instead of building great shrines, like Notre Dame, with its womb-like doors. All great churches have pussy-shaped doors. Some brick churches down South have doors about as appealing as the guillotine. The little churches of the colored folk have given me my closest religion, the music of the great R&B artists.

Noticing that they were both naked might be shocking, but the "sin" of it is they must have felt instinctively that they could procreate. The knowledge of creation/existence might be the sin itself. The serpent knew what would cause humans to kill. I still have the rattlers my sister sent me of a snake she killed. It seemed the right thing to do in Kansas--kill the serpent, the lowest form of the temptation. We humans have a history of wholesale killings of everything and ourselves. Maybe that assuages our ambiguity of existence. While an animal kills without that knowledge, man might be stuck with the idea that someone else can take his place, at least temporarily, and temporary is all we got, like it or not. As the Carter Family sings, "Everybody got to walk that Lonesome Valley/Nobody here can walk it for you. You got to walk it by yourself."

SUBJECT: Re: Against the fear of death

Mark Twain must have read Lucretius. He said, "I do not fear death. I had been dead for billions and billions of years before I was born, and had not suffered the slightest inconvenience from it." Lucretius wrote, "Look back also and see how the ages of everlasting time past before we were born have been to us nothing. This therefore is a mirror which nature holds up to us, showing the time to come after we at length shall die. Is there anything horrible in that? Is there anything gloomy? Is it not more peaceful than any sleep?" One hopes.

I didn't like the policy of "submissions". Ha! I always printed the stuff I wanted to. Allen didn't like the word "stuff". I didn't like his word "poesy".

Ginsberg's life work was to make sure people will remember his name. I introduced him at a reading at Johns Hopkins saying, "Drop your socks and grab your cocks, here's Allen Ginsberg!" He seemed embarrassed, but I reminded him later that one of his tactics was to shock his audience...like stripping naked at Columbia University.

Ginsberg heard about Wichita through me, and in some of those photos of me and him and Larry, I have a Bob Branaman drawing in my hand. I was showing his work to Larry and Allen. The proof is in those pictures. Branaman is probably the one who told Ginsberg the vortex myth of the "hicks", Bruce Connors and Michael McClure, who liked to say they couldn't get away from Wichita. Allen liked to repeat it and he idealized those two, and so did Ferlinghetti. It was very competitive in the poetry/art sphere then. I didn't join any clique, nor cared too much for where I was or who I knew. It was *Life* and *Time* magazines who created my fame, that I was in the middle of everyone, when everyone wanted a piece of what was happening. Allen took me to meet Larry at his house up on Potrero Hill. Larry served us wine and cheese, and as we left, Allen said, "Y'know, Larry isn't really that good a poet."

SUBJECT: Money bombs

Keep the government's hands off of drugs. Too late now, I guess. Drugs were legal in my grandparents' day. Obviously, people want them. Something about that runs through us. You say, people cannot take care of themselves, it's "existential"? Yeah, so was Dick Tracy.

The country was taken over by the biggest criminal of all time, and a couple pays a half million dollars for their daughter to score high enough to get into a worthless college. There is insanity all around. And once again, Christ, a black man's life was squeezed out of him by the police while the country watched. Too much information, not enough truth. Meanwhile, the grifter grinds.

It reminds me when I taught a short story course at the University of Maryland. Being virtually illiterate, I found an anthology of short stories to read that contained one of Hemmingway's. I liked it. It also had one by Stephen Crane about some people on an island (stranded) while a passenger ship passed by. The people on the island started waving for their life. The people on the ship waved their enthusiastic greetings and passed on. I used that as a "picture" of existentialism. That course had an overflowing enrollment so they put us in in the Physics building adjacent to campus. There were lots of foreign students in there, studying science. One walked past as I stood at the doorway. He looked at the class and noticed it was all women. He asked me what the course was, and I replied, "women studies". He walked on with puzzled look.

Mike Watt has my "Planet Chernobyl" poem set to come out next year, as an opera. He's turned the poem into a libretto, with Petra Haden singing my words. She's added violin and mandolin to Mike's bass, and given the whole thing a new sort of country sound. The Chernobyl accident happened on my 51st birthday--April 26, 1986--but it wasn't after I read Svetlana Alexievich's *Voices of Chernobyl: The Oral History of a Nuclear Disaster* a few years ago that I began to put my words to it all. I used to think Allen was "off" with his nuclear power protests, his trying to stop trains full of nuclear waste and stuff. Back then I wasn't behind Allen, but now I see how nuclear power can kill us all. After reading that book, I couldn't rest. Strange times now. News from the border tonight: nineteen thousand children taking turns sleeping on the floor.

SUBJECT: Re: Fw: memoires from Sue

Funny the small child memories we have. I remember my parents taking me and my sister to the World's Fair out here. We went to a performance by a burlesque dancer. I think it was Sally Rand and her fan dance, unless I have that part mixed up. I remember blurting out, "She's beautiful", and people laughed. My mother blushed in embarrassment and my father smiled. That is my earliest full childhood memory.

I'm far removed from any lit/music activity, which is probably changing a lot, as everything is, post shit-storm 2020. The only ones I know left are Miriam at Norton, Nicca Ray and Benito, and, of course, Mike Watt in Pedro. I don't know what Byron Coley is doing in Northampton now. Last time I saw Byron was at his all-July party with Kim Gordon, et al, and Bill Nace who recorded my "Apocalypse Rose" poem for Guillaume Belhomme at Lenka Lente, a French publisher.

I think the word "sauntering" comes from the activity of kids taunting the bums begging for coins outside a church, St. Teresa or something al la St. Tierra. I'm not sure where I got that story, but I remember when I was printing *Zap* in San Francisco a kid came over and wanted me to meet a new band with funny name that he was manager of--Pink Floyd. I wonder who that kid was now. I don't remember that, either.

Get it? Got it? Good? Go, man, go! "Time is tight."

SUBJECT: Re: Fw: LOVE LOVE #4

We might now be in a crisis too big. Too many years of ignorance and violence. After all, there's a town in Colorado named after the Union officer who slaughtered the women and children of Black Kettle's tribe and cut out their privates to decorate saddle horns. The soldiers cut off the women's breasts so they could be sewed up and sold as novelty purses on Turk Street. They bashed out the toddlers' brains with horse hooves. The Sand Creek Massacre. How can a country live down that kind of karma? These are the same "good people" who killed off the buffalo and everything else in sight, plowed up the prairie grass so much to cause dust storms. That's just the beginning. The meth head insurgency and the gun violence reveal the deep criminal mind that's evolved in this country's consciousness. We had a chance being "the greatest generation", but that has been lost. We have become the enemy we fought.

I don't write much anymore and I can't find my dream notes without you. Here's something I wrote this morning after reading your email. You can use it... or not. Makes no difference to me. Love Love.

(A corruption of Woody Guthrie, in whose same dust storm I was born.)

>This country was their land
>not our land, from California
>to New York Island, from the
>Redwood forest to Gulf Stream waters
>this land was stolen for you and me.
>
>We have built this country
>running booze and dope, from clipper ships,
>from sleek speed boats, and blamed
>it on the other fools. Our manifest
>became orange-ized crime
>and our government followed suit.
>We loved the mobster movies,
>drove off or flew away with hit men souls.

SUBJECT: Re: Drugs

I'm reading *Empire of Pain*, about the Sackler family and their marketing of drugs. It's pretty interesting so far, but there's one inconsistency: he says the opioid crisis didn't start until the introduction of oxycontin. Wrong. How about the heroin deaths in the black communities? When those drugs were criminalized in 1914, a lot of the people using them were suddenly cut off. Initially, there were clinics, allowed by the government, where people were able to keep getting their drugs, but then there was a moral hysteria. There's always been moral hysteria about drugs in America.

I remember reading that Samuel Taylor Coleridge, the poet who wrote "Kubla Khan", went to a chemist for a big bottle of laudanum to get in bed for the winter. The chemist said it was a good idea. It reads like a laudanum poem. The closest thing to that I knew was the turpine hydrate and codeine that Ray Bremser and I used to hit the drug stores for. It felt better than anything. The only methadone I've had is what Burroughs gave me in Lawrence on that visit with Billy, when I was sick, the stuff he said, "would kick in on the other side of Kansas City." It did and Billy drove all the way to Kentucky.

I have a great book on criminals of 1800s. There's a story in it of a guy who went to an opium den on Mott Street, in New York City, and tried the pipe on two or three different occasions, but he only got a headache and never went back. Ironically, he laid out his street clothes with billfold, money, etc., before he went to lay with the pipe and they were never touched by the others who frequented the parlor. Maybe they ought to bring back opium to stop petty crimes. Laws, again, are the problem, not the drugs. Ginsberg used to sit up at his farm and clip *New York Times* articles about the military bringing opium back in body bags. I'm sure the army contractors are bringing back tons easily now in cargo planes. Twenty years in Afghanistan has moved a lot of dope. No doubt the Mexicans on the southern border are a smokescreen for political money. Pointing fingers, saying there's a threat, is what that's all about that. Was it Benjamin Franklin who said the Constitution was a good idea if we can keep it? It looks like it's up for grabs now, to the meth-head insurrectionists and whoever has the biggest guns. It was a better country, or more honest at least, when people could go to the pharmacy and get a bottle of Bayer

Heroin. My grandmother needed it to get through the desolation and terror of the Territory. Even our bennies in the '50s were more honest, until someone put the Benzedrine in Mrs. Murphy's Ovaltine!

I wear dead men's clothes for the most part. I still have a beautiful gray Pierre Cardin shirt I got from Goodwill when we lived in D.C. area. It must have belonged to a pimp, or politician on the lam. I wear it with matching gray silk scarf from a Sioux Indian I met at pow wow along Chisholm Trail. I scored a pinstriped suit with thin gray stripes there, too. When Pam was working for The Wall Street Journal in D.C. and I was teaching in Jessup Prison,"The Cut", the WSJ had a big party and the Dow Jones president from New York City came. I wore the pinstripe with some boots I bought in Tijuana a long time ago. Those fit like a glove. I told the salesperson in Tijuana to give my Florshiems away. I painted them white as they got older. There I was, white boots and pinstripe suit, with the Dow Jones people wanting to know who the new billionaire was. It was 1980 or so. They expected conformity at Dow Jones then.

SUBJECT: Re: Never seen anything like this before

I hope they nail the criminally insane soon. Not so sure about the timeline. He's no longer a scar on the Constitution, he's a festering wound. Virus and climate change on top of it all. We are living in a horror movie. They called it karma in the '60s. I do think that Trump will get his due. At the very least, I hope he gets so politically scarred that he won't be able to run in 2024, and the equally criminal Republicans who make their home up his ass will finally cut the umbilical cord. Criminals running free, right-wing enablers, stupid uneducated voters, racism, all wrapped into one ball of shit.

The students are right. War has become whatever propaganda says it is. The Taliban's got nothing on Reverend Chivington, the Union colonel whose troops crushed babies under horse hooves at Sands Creek. I knew Tucker Carlson's dad, Dick Carlson, when we had our press on Mission. I think it was Ackerman's partner who was friends with him. Anyway, they had a little van with a tire painted on the side of it; they were freelance reporters masquerading as a tire changing service. In the round hole of the painted-on tire rim, they had a camera trying to get shots, photos, they could use in their political stories.

SUBJECT: Inscribed book

The guy who bought it, Arthur Nusbaum, has Third Mind Books. He takes the Burroughs/Plymell cut-ups to Burroughs panels and conferences, like the one I was on at CUNY. I talked about Burroughs' love of guns and they quickly went on to something else. Media fed brains won't pay attention to what's not in the script. Nusbaum got those cut-ups when he came by and gave me five grand for my little bookcase full of signed books. I didn't mean to include Gerard's book, but I guess now we're even because I think Gerard sold my *The Trashing of America* that I inscribed to him. Also in that bookcase were two pages of original typescripts from Burroughs of our collaboration cut-ups from 1963. I had put them between covers of a catalogue for safe keeping and forgot they were there.

I never cared for the Warhol Factory crowd. A bunch of stupid squares who stumbled onto "Pop". Someone told Warhol to paint the can realistically. I thought they were a bunch of stupid girls playing make up and the conversation was a terrific bore. I still have your mystery rocks and the sculpture pieces I made to hold the male and female rocks, but I can't put them in the sculptures except for an exhibit because of the reaction between the rocks and the metal. I think those have more to say than anything Warhol ever did.

SUBJECT: Re: Champion Jack Dupree CDs.

I done wondering where he be. Thank you. Those CDs brought the '50s back to me. I was drivin' that beautiful chick to Joplin, Missouri in my '49 Pontiac with radio on playin' Hank Ballard. Later, she took me for a sucker and left me in a bar. I played the piano to no one there, tryin' to be just like Jack Dupree. I wonder how much he influenced Jerry Lee? Or even the Fat Man? The greatest in R&B comes from the boogie beat. She left me for another guy and I had to sleep alone in Joplin. I think her name was Voss. Jimmy Mammy tried to steal her and Ronnie Wikel, too. Her dad was in the soda pop business in Wichita, I think. Nobody left who might know, except maybe Branaman.

My W-Words may piss off the liberal establishment. It takes up the double referent I found in *Semantics*, a book written by my old friend Hugh Walpole. My essay has a semantic evaluation of the n-word in it, which is acceptable, is it not? I guess "not". We liberated the f-word. Now f'ing is acceptable on TV. People took ownership of speech on the n-word. That never works. Maybe too late for intelligence. It's changing fast here.

LOVESICK BLUES OR SICK LOVE BLUES

Melancholia of spirit of sunset
involution paralysis of those
who sing for their souls.

The sound of a motor
on a hill far away
going somewhere.

Even a moonscape blowing
precious moments wild frontier.
Saints leading their ponies
through the gold dust.

Time Whip!

A jubilee in the mounds of time
existentialism handcuffed freedom
digging hell of the hole
revved up in a skin of brakes.

Drain and gurgle of language
seed crop of addled masses
flush the clichéd speech in
self-inflicted wounds of the
pubic cubes blown out asses.
Digital Age entanglements in
Morphic Resonance publics
spooks of Mr. In-Between

SUBJECT: Merle and Neal

Kip told me a while back that Merle Haggard and Neal Cassady were locked up in San Quentin at the same time. It turns out Merle served two years, from March 1958 until March 1960, and Neal served two years, from May 1958 until May 1960, so they were there, at the same time, for 20 months. The prison held around 3,100 inmates then, but there's no way to tell if Merle and Neal knew each other. Kip just found an interview Al Aronowitz did with Neal at San Quentin, with Neal mentioning his having an Okie cellmate: "The rules say you get five to life for selling marijuana. That's the same as an armed robber gets or a hypo? You know, a junkie who has to take his narcotics with a hypodermic needle. That's the same as what a man gets for going out on the street and threatening another man's life with a gun. So here I am in a cell with an Okie armed robber. He'll probably spend less time here than I will."

I never asked Neal, dammit, but it had to be Merle. The person who would have known for sure is Gavin Arthur, the grandson of President Chester Arthur, but he's long gone. He was Neal's teacher/mentor in prison. Neal and his Anne and I went to Gavin's place near Gough Street. Gavin was kind of a seer. There was a snippet about him in the *San Francisco Chronicle* once, Gavin saying his friends were appalled when he voted for Nixon but he "knew" the next president would die in office. That was Nixon/Kennedy, 1960.

SUBJECT: JAM THE THROTTLE SKIPPER LARRY, Final draft

JAM THE THROTTLE SKIPPER LARRY
(SOS To Ensign Ferlinghetti of the Greatest Generation)

I think I've figured you out now Larry,
Your aloofness, looking aside to avoid intimacy
directness, indifferent, a literary lion in the S.F. hills.
Only getting in a conversation when a topic met
your interest, maybe grumbling about the tab
when too many poets were at the table.
Thanks for taking me & Pam to Mike's Pool Hall,
She was under age, but with you, respected
business man, no questions asked, long bar with
best food, the Salami Factory next door, with
San Francisco sourdough (they say the "mother"
came there on a wagon train). Old Italian men at
the tables studying the pool play, checkered table
cloths, Caruso on the juke box, a great cappuccino
on occasion at Cafe Trieste, your fabulous
North Beach in the day. Before GoGo got there
and gone, I got to visit other literary lions, too:
Rexroth, took Allen on my motorcycle to see
Patchen, first met you when Allen introduced us
at your home where you reclined in bed, offered
wine, and as we left, Allen said you were not
that good a poet, but you sure were able-bodied
one of the best minds of your generation, a "ninety
day wonder" the sailors or snobs may have said
while sipping martinis at the Top of The Mark
watching your ship sail under the Golden Gate.
"Just kids" they may have said as the seagulls flew
into the peace of the sky and you sailed into Hell.
Kids they were, washing their skivvies and hanging
Them to dry while trying to keep the collar starched,
the tie straight, the commander's cap on just right.

I asked if you wanted to go with me & Pam to see
Neal off on the bus with Tom Wolfe, Kesey and the
Pranksters, not interested, and when you came to my
Gough Street party with Allen, Whalen, McClure, et al,
where Beats met Hippies, wild LSD dances happening,
you stood alone looking indifferent at the scene, aloof
offered conversation only when someone engaged you.
I bet I know why... a mild case of PTSD? They called
it "shell shocked" then, if not from shells, certainly the
shock of witnessing Nagasaki, immediately then a pacifist,
saw humanity and all living creatures in a different light,
like others, never to talk about the war, especially among
other beatnik poets, intellectuals, and the like. Hell you
could have shown the judge the photo of you as commander
and said, "Sorry, that's the way we talked in the war", but it was
the model of how to sell copies, howling about free speech.
You became a Francophile, met Mary Beach put in internment
Camp when Nazis invaded Paris, a photo of her with your boss,
Ike, after the war with his hand on her backside (upper in the photo).
I take back all the bad things I've said about you. Who cares about
the little royalties. Honored to have you publish my poem in City
Lights Journal and my first book. You came over to our pad to help
Neal get his book together with Allen and published him instead of
another book by Kerouac. Allen did the lit talk. Neal rolled a joint.
You sat quietly as usual, maybe remembering the dark waves
rising up like ship's hulls at Normandy. You lived a long life.
(Navy chow?) Saw the perverted power begin other atrocities
the Big Lie of Viet Nam. The Big Lie of the Gulf War, invading
sovereign countries and killing their leaders, Capitalistic Lies
for greed and avarice, oil, dope, derivatives, dark money, guns. etc.
And now the Big Lie again when you lay dying. Ironically, we fell
under the Third Reich's "Lie repeated often enough becomes the truth"
that you fought against. The criminal madman again with trouble using
the language, literature unknown, but able to gain power telling The Lie
for the ignorant hypocrites, fundamentalists, meth head Insurrectionists.

We used to ask, "Where were the citizens who listened to Brahms
                                                                  & read Goethe"
that let a criminally insane madman become the leader.
Now we are again in that peril, the crises in the world you fought against.
SOS Larry, help save our souls, save our ships, wherever you are.

From Charley: Both Billy the Kid and Custer were losers. Billy the Kid is using a machine gun (Tommy gun) that was quickly outlawed in the '30s when gangsters got the drop on cops. If the government outlawed fully automatic guns then, why don't they ban assault rifles today?

Charley Plymell at his computer with Herbert

Photo © 2023 by Mark Reinertson

About Charles Plymell

Charles Plymell was born in a converted chicken coop in Holcomb, Kansas in 1935, the same year as Jerry Lee Lewis and Elvis Presley, but neither of them were born in a dust storm, and neither them had a mother who went out and shot rabbits and gathered cactus for food. He comes from a unique set of circumstances. Plymell can trace his family origins to the settlers of the Jamestown, Virginia colony and to the indigenous Cherokee tribes who were forced from their homes and into Oklahoma Territory. He recited his first poem at age 4, in the back of a truck on his way to California. At age 15, Plymell left high school in San Antonio, Texas in a new 1951 Chevrolet his dad bought for him and drove it back to Wichita, Kansas. As he recalls it, "That fall, I was about to go into my sophomore year, but then I woke up. I had a new car, gas was 15¢ a gallon. I could lie about my age, get a job anywhere and start doing anything I wanted. I put that high school in my rear-view mirror. There was nothing there, just a bunch of squares playing football."

Plymell got jobs working on post-war "infrastructure" projects across the American West, building roads, pipelines and dams. He also fell into the jazz/R&B club scene in Wichita, a place fueled by Benzedrine, brimming with new fashions and a new sound. A night in jail with artist friend Bob Branaman led Plymell to take classes at Wichita University, which connected him to a new set of cohorts who later became part of the San Francisco art and poetry scene. When he moved to San Francisco in 1962, Plymell took over the lease on a seven-bedroom flat on Gough Street, previously home to a series of Wichita writers and also the place where Allen Ginsberg had written "Howl". A house party, some meth, some LSD, and Plymell soon found himself welcoming Ginsberg and Neal Cassady into his world as his new roommates, as they set about writing out Cassady's memoir "The First Third" under the supervision of Lawrence Ferlinghetti.

Plymell's knowledge of printing led him to create a series of underground magazines while he was in San Francisco, including *Zap Comics* with R. Crumb and *Now* with Philip Whalen, and Glenn Todd.

At the same time, Plymell was making himself known as a writer, with David Haselwood's Auerhahn Press publishing his poem "Apocalypse Rose" in 1967. While working on the docks in 1969, Plymell was recruited by two students of Eliott Coleman's to go to Coleman's famed writing seminars at Johns Hopkins University. After arriving in Baltimore, Plymell began work on *Last of the Mocassins* as his Masters' thesis. His degree led Plymell into a teaching career, where he provided guidance on literature and writing at various East Coast colleges and prisons, while also collaborating with John Giorno to produce *The Trashing of America*, a now rare and much-sought after poetry collection.

A road trip to Cherry Valley, New York, to the northeast of Cooperstown, led Plymell to buy property there in the early 1970s. After settling into the store buildings where Samuel Morse first created his code, he continued to print and publish underground magazines featuring the work of his friends and visitors, including Roxie Powell, Charles Henri Ford, Joshua Norton, Carl Solomon, William Burroughs, James Grauerholz, Gerard Malanga, and Mary Beach. Today, at 88, Plymell still lives in Cherry Valley with his wife, Pam, and a menagerie of feral cats. He stays in contact with people around the world, and encourages independent thinking, daily, by email.

Plymell thrives in the underground, as a wizard of words, a beacon of mischief and a master of making connections. In 1955, he wrote the lines "shuffle on down slide away from the mass/wanna smiz zoke a jiz zoint of griz zass?" in closing out a poem describing a night out in Wichita, doing Benzedrine and smoking weed. That line predates the arrival of "the Beats" by a few years, Snoop Dogg by 40, and Plymell still smokes pot. In Martin Scorsese's 2019 documentary *Rolling Thunder Revue*, Allen Ginsberg credits Plymell as being the one who introduced him to Bob Dylan's music.

COLOPHON

Keyboard Intercourse was designed by
Bill Roberts and published in October, 2023.

The text is set in 12 & 14 point Adobe Jenson Pro.

This first printing is limited to
an edition of 126 copies;
100 in wraps &
26 hardbound copies.

www.ingramcontent.com/pod-product-compliance
Lightning Source LLC
Chambersburg PA
CBHW060215050426
42446CB00013B/3076